春雨惊春清谷天
夏满芒夏暑相连
秋处露秋寒霜降
冬雪雪冬小大寒

本教材为 2016 年度教育部哲学社会科学研究重大课题攻关项目
“中国书法文化国际传播的理论与实践研究”（16JZD031) 阶段性成果

二十四节气

夏

風調雨順

Summer: Season with Timely Breeze and Rain for Crop Raising

The Twenty-four Solar Terms

主编：周斌 周佳楠
Editor-in-chief: ZHOU Bin, ZHOU Jianan

副主编：Roy Ye 尹冬民
Associate Editor: Roy Ye, YIN Dongmin

插图：孙凌雁
Illustrator:SUN Lingyan

书法：盛兰军
Calligraphy: SHENG Lanjun

翻译：吴顺俪 Misti McDaniel
Translators: WU Shunli, Misti McDaniel

封面题字：Roy Ye
Calligraphy on the cover: Roy Ye

华东师范大学出版社

Nini, it is May 5th today.
Happy birthday to you.

Jerry, I find out that I am a Taurus according to the astrological signs. Do you know? My birthday is during the period of Beginning of Summer according to the Twenty-four Solar Terms. That is when spring is over and summer time begins. Let me tell you the stories about the summer solar terms.

妮妮，今天是5月5号，祝你生日快乐！

杰瑞，我按照星座图查到了我是金牛座，你知道吗？我的生日正好在立夏时节，现在春天已经结束，进入夏季了，让我来给你讲讲夏季的节气故事。

二十四节气与十二星座对照图

The table of the Twenty-four Solar Terms and the corresponding astrological signs

Contents

The Symphony of Summer

目 录

夏季乐章

立夏

Beginning of Summer

Li Xia

The story of **Beginning of Summer**

Important facts about Beginning of Summer

Beginning of Summer, which is also called “Li Xia”, is the first Solar term of summer. It is between 5th and 7th May every year. After Beginning of Summer, the temperature begins to rise and crops begin to grow. The regions south of the Yangtze River start to enter the rainy season. It rains continuously and the temperature changes frequently.

Changes after Beginning of Summer

Mole crickets sing, earthworms dig the ground.
Wheat stalks begin to sprout and melon vines grow.
Locust trees and Chinese roses are in blossom.

立夏大事记

立夏是夏季的第一个节气，时间点是在每年的5月5～7日之间。立夏时节，气温显著升高，农作物生长旺盛，农业生产进入农忙时节。江南地区开始进入雨季，阴雨绵绵，气温多变。

立夏变化

蝼蛄鸣叫，蚯蚓掘土。
小麦扬花，王瓜爬藤。
槐花绽放，月季盛开。

跟着妮妮学一学
Learning Chinese calligraphy with Nini

篆书 (zhuan shu) | Seal script

“立”字的本义是“站立”。篆书“立”的字形像一个人分开两腿，站立在地上。

“立” means “to stand”. The seal script of “立” resembles a man standing straight on the ground with his legs apart.

篆书“夏”字的中间是“页”部，表示人的头部，左右两旁表示双手，下方表示双足，整体像一个高大威猛的人。后借指中国第一个朝代夏朝，又指四季中的夏季。

The middle part in the seal script of “夏” is the radical “页”, which means the head of a human being. The left and right parts in the seal script indicate the two hands and the bottom part indicates the two feet. The whole character looks like a tall and strong man. It is later used to indicate the first dynasty in Chinese history, Xia Dynasty and is also used to mean summer in the four seasons.

跟着杰瑞写一写

Practicing calligraphy with Jerry

楷书 (kai shu) | Regular script

在学写"立夏"之前，我们先来学习书法中一些常见的基本笔画。之后大家可以举一反三进行练习。

Before we start writing "立夏", let's learn some fundamental strokes in Chinese calligraphy first. Then you will be able to apply them to your later practice.

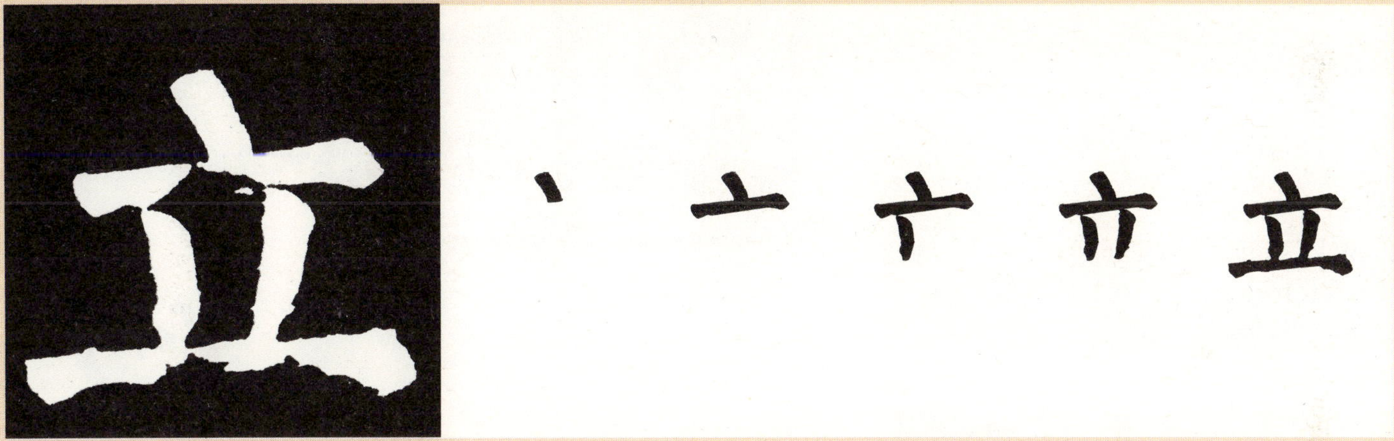

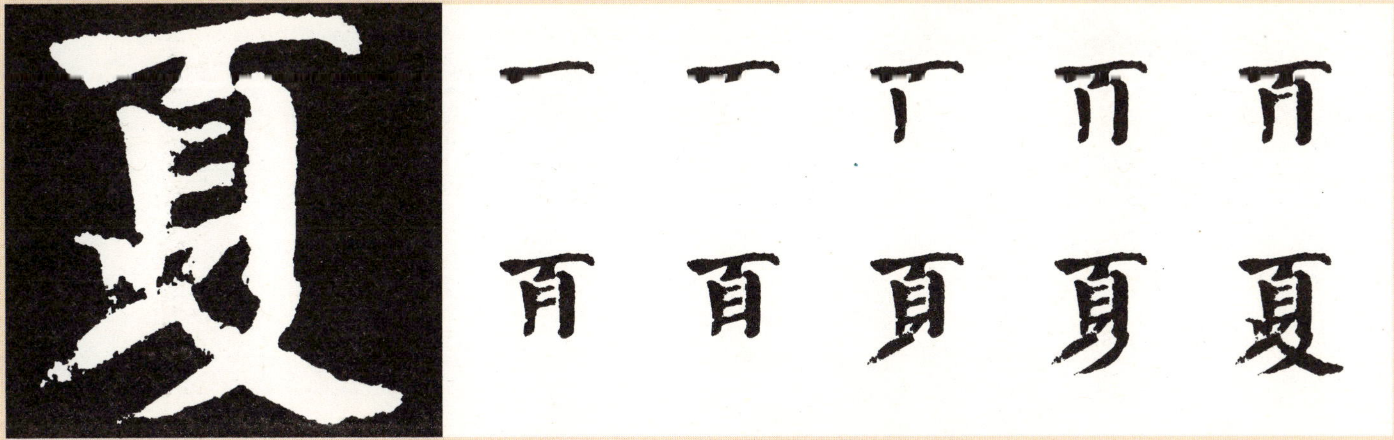

Make a gift with Chinese characters “立夏”

剪剪画画
做立夏的礼物

跟着妮妮和杰瑞
做送给朋友的
礼物

Let’s make some gifts for our friends with Nini and Jerry

剪一剪、画一画

Paper cutting and graphic design

Paper cutting by Nini
妮妮的剪纸

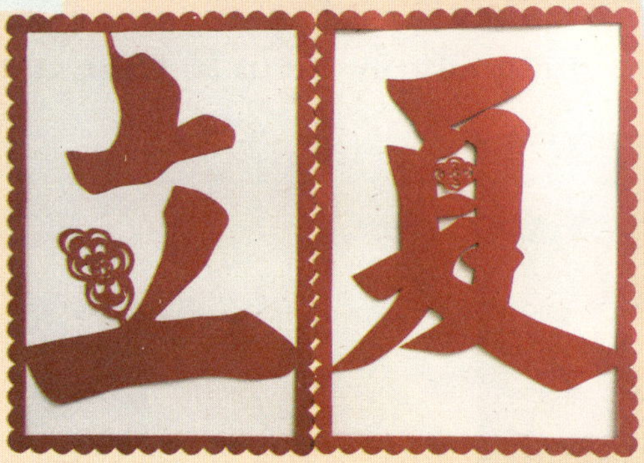

Graphic designed by Jerry
杰瑞的画

猜一猜、说一说

Let's make a guess

Let's make a guess with Nini and Jerry

与妮妮和杰瑞一起猜一猜

与“立夏”对应的是哪个星座？

Which astrological sign corresponds to Beginning of Summer?

Let's have a competition with Nini and Jerry

与妮妮和杰瑞一起比赛

说出与“夏”有关的词语

Try to say as many words as you can that are relevant to“夏”

小满

Lesser Fullness

Xiao Man

Important facts about Lesser Fullness

The story of **Lesser Fullness**

Lesser Fullness comes between May 20th and 22nd every year. Lesser Fullness means that, during this period of time, crops grow the most and grains start to mature. After Lesser Fullness, the weather gradually becomes hotter and the difference of the temperature between the south and the north of China becomes smaller and smaller. Silkworms start to make silk cocoons.

Changes after Lesser Fullness

Sow thistle flourishes. Grass withers.
The wheat begins mature gradually.
Pomegranate flowers are in bloom.
Migrating birds make their way back to the north.
Rains become abundant.

小满的故事

小满大事记

小满的时间点在每年的5月20～22日之间。小满是指此时的农作物都生长得比较茂盛，谷物的籽粒开始变得饱满。小满过后天气渐渐炎热，南北温差缩小，蚕开始吐丝结茧。

小满变化

苦菜茂盛，靡草枯萎。
麦粒渐满，石榴花开。
候鸟北归，雨水丰盈。

跟着妮妮学一学
Learning Chinese calligraphy with Nini

篆书 (zhuan shu) | Seal script

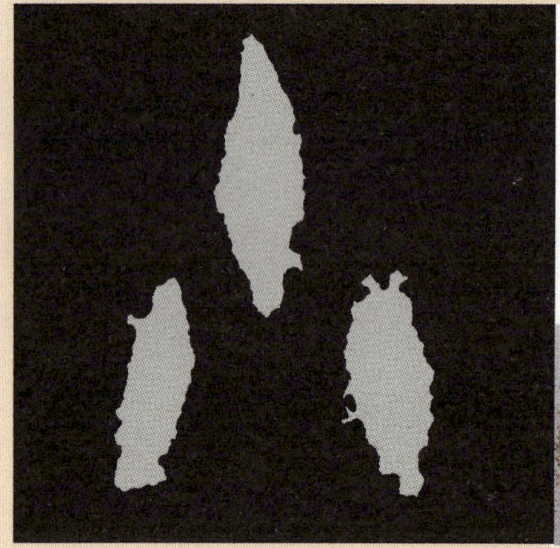

篆书“小”字从字形上看像数颗细小的沙粒散落四周，表示细小、细微的意思。

The seal script of “小” resembles several tiny grains of sand scattered around, which indicates smallness or subtlety.

篆书“满”字是左形右声，左边的“水”是形旁，右边是声旁，“满”指液体灌满容器每一处并外溢。

The seal script of “满” is composed of two characters. The left radical “水” stands for the meaning and the right radical stands for the sound. The whole character literally means liquid fills every part of the container and spills out.

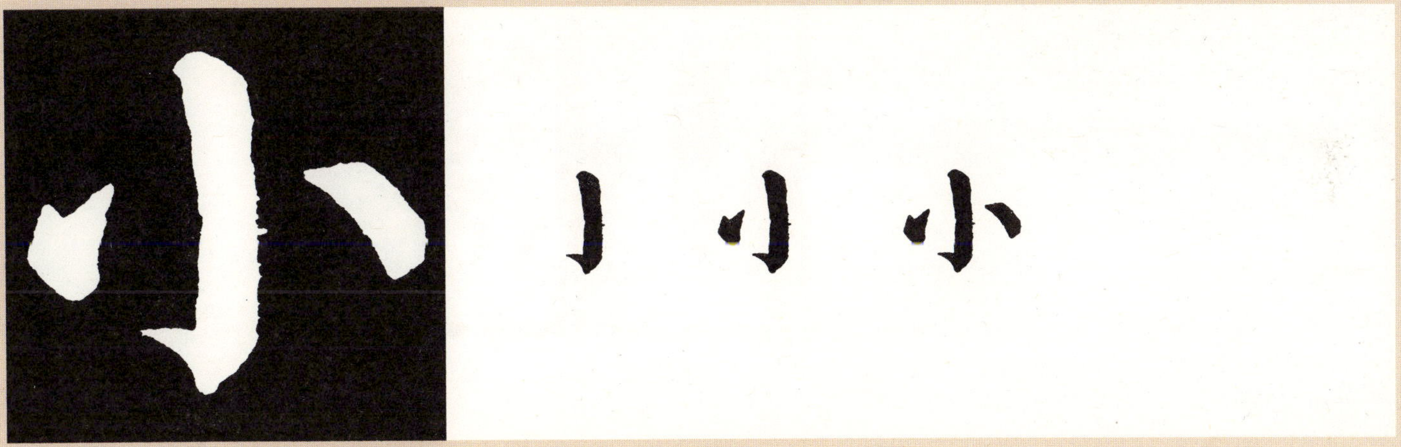

剪一剪、画一画

Paper cutting and graphic design

Make a gift with Chinese characters “小满”

剪剪画画

做小满的礼物

跟着妮妮和杰瑞做送给朋友的礼物

Let’s make some gifts for our friends with Nini and Jerry

Paper cutting by Nini

妮妮的剪纸

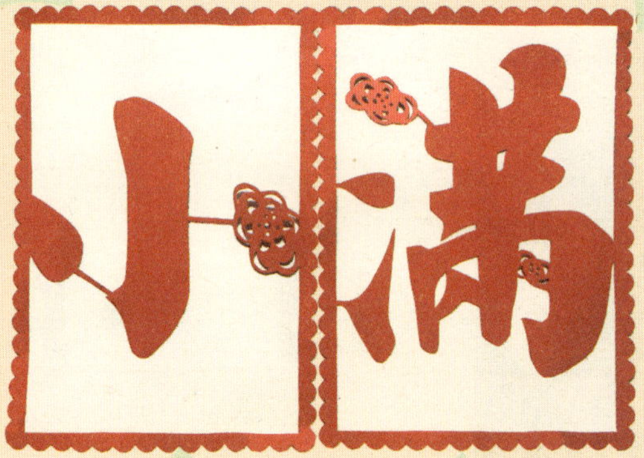

Graphic designed by Jerry

杰瑞的画

猜一猜、说一说

Let's make a guess

Let's make a guess with Nini and Jerry

与妮妮和杰瑞一起猜一猜

与"小满"对应
的是哪个星座?

Which astrological sign corresponds
to Lesser Fullness?

Let's have a competition with Nini and Jerry

与妮妮和杰瑞一起比赛

说出与"满"
有关的词语

Try to say as many words as you can
that are relevant to "满"

芒种

Grain in Ear
Mang Zhong

The story of **Grain in Ear**

Important facts about Grain in Ear

Grain in Ear, "Mang Zhong" in Chinese, comes between 5th and 7th June every year. Grain in Ear means that the crops, such as wheat, barley, etc. are ready for harvest. The crops that are planted in summer, such as rice, are ready to sow. "芒种"shares a similar pronunciation with "忙种" in Chinese, which means "busy sowing". This indicates farmers are in their busiest time of the year. It rains a lot during this period and the temperature rises significantly. The regions south of the Yangtze River start to enter the Plum Rain season because plums become mature and ripe.

Changes after Grain in Ear

Mantis' eggs hatch. Shrikes start to sing.
Wheat is harvested and rice is planted.
It is time for competing in Dragon Boat Races.
People feast on the triangle-shaped rice dumplings during the Dragon Boat Festival.

芒种大事记

芒种的时间点在每年的6月5～7日之间。芒种是指小麦、大麦等有芒的农作物已经成熟，可以收割；水稻等夏季播种的农作物可以播种。“芒种”谐音为“忙种”，预示着农民进入了一年中最忙碌的时节。芒种时节雨量充沛，气温显著升高，江南地区开始进入“梅雨季节”。

芒种变化

蝗螂破卵，伯劳始鸣。
麦子收割，水稻栽秧。
龙船竞渡，端午食粽。

The Dragon Boat Festival is on May 5th on Lunar Calendar, which is an important traditional festival for Chinese people. Since Ancient Times, there have been many customs for this festival, such as competing in Dragon Boat races, hanging calamus and wormwood leaves in the house, eating triangle-shaped rice dumplings, drinking realgar wine, etc. Children wear five-colored ropes to keep themselves safe and healthy. People also commemorate the great ancient Chinese poet Qu Yuan.

eating triangle-shaped rice dumplings

competing in Dragon Boat races

端午节

农历的五月初五是端午节，它是中国民间重要的传统节日。自古以来在端午节便有很多节日风俗，比如赛龙舟、在家里悬挂菖蒲和艾草、吃粽子、饮雄黄酒等。孩子们会在这一天系上五彩绳，以保安康。同时人们会在端午节这天纪念中国古代伟大的诗人屈原。

吃粽了

赛龙舟

篆书 (zhuan shu) | Seal script

“芒”字的篆书由“艸”和“亡”组成，是上形下声。它的本义是谷类植物种子壳上或草木上的针状物。

The seal script of “芒” consists of “艸”and “亡”, with the upper part standing for the meaning and the bottom part standing for the sound. It means the needles on the shells of seeds of grain or the herbs.

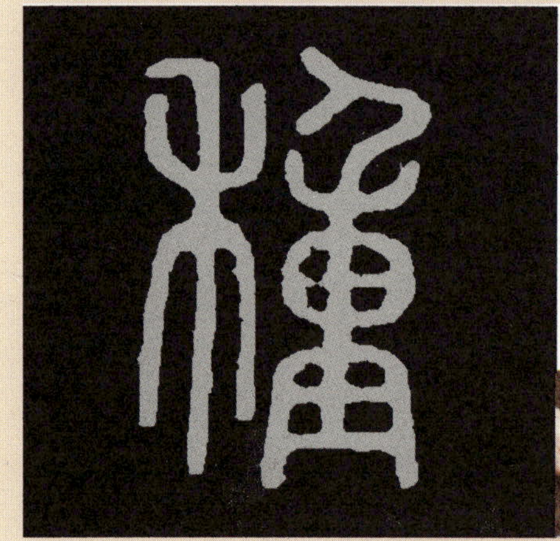

篆书“种”字由“禾”和“重”组合而成，是左形右声。它的意思是把种子或幼苗等埋在泥土里使它生长。

The seal script of “种” consists of “禾” and “重”, with the left part standing for the meaning and the right part standing for the sound. It means to plant seeds or seedling in the soil to let them grow.

楷书 (kai shu) | Regular script

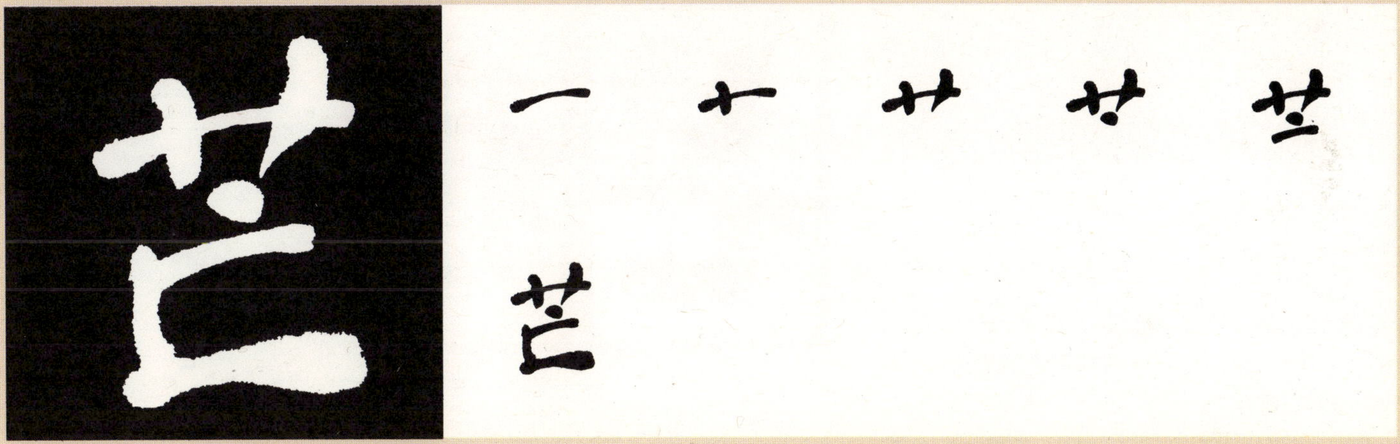

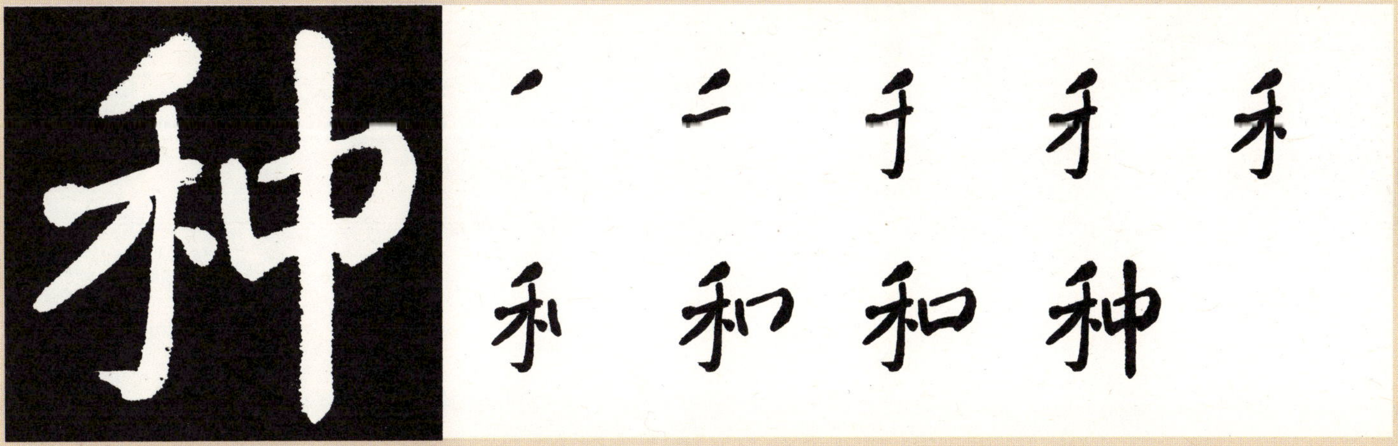

Make a gift with Chinese characters “芒种”

剪剪画画 做芒种的礼物

跟着妮妮和杰瑞做送给朋友的礼物

Let’s make some gifts for our friends with Nini and Jerry

剪一剪、画一画

Paper cutting and graphic design

Paper cutting by Nini
妮妮的剪纸

Graphic designed by Jerry
杰瑞的画

猜一猜、说一说

Let's make a guess

Let's make a guess with Nini and Jerry

与妮妮和杰瑞一起猜一猜

与“芒种”对应的是哪个星座？

Which astrological sign corresponds to Grain in Ear?

Let's have a competition with Nini and Jerry

与妮妮和杰瑞一起比赛

说出与“种”有关的词语

Try to say as many words as you can that are relevant to “种”

夏至

Summer Solstice
Xia Zhi

The story of **Summer Solstice**

Important facts about Summer Solstice

Summer Solstice, “Xia Zhi” in Chinese, comes between 21st and 22nd June every year. Summer Solstice marks the longest day of the whole year in the Northern Hemisphere. It indicates the hottest season of the year starts and after that every day will get hotter and hotter. During this period of time, there is ample sunshine and crops flourish.

Changes after Summer Solstice

Deer shed their antlers. Cicadas cry continuously.

Plums ripen. Gardenias are in blossoms.

The wheat is put in the barn. Farmers are busy hoeing the weed.

夏至大事记

夏至的时间点在每年的6月21～22日之间。夏至是北半球全年中白昼时间最长的一天，之后白天逐渐变短。它预示着一年中最炎热的时节正式开始，之后的天气将越来越炎热。此时日照充足，农作物生长十分旺盛。

夏至变化

鹿角脱落，蝉鸣不停。
梅子黄熟，栀子花开。
麦子归仓，锄草正忙。

篆书 (zhuan shu) | Seal script

篆书"夏"字的中间是"页"部，表示人的头部，左右两旁表示双手，下方表示双足，整体像一个高大威猛的人。后借指中国第一个朝代夏朝，又指四季中的夏季。

The middle part in the seal script of "夏" is the radical "页", which means the head of a human being. The left and right parts in the seal script indicate the two hands and the bottom part indicates the two feet. The whole character looks like a tall and strong man. It is later used to indicate the first dynasty in China's history, Xia Dynasty and is also used to mean summer in the four seasons.

篆书"至"是会意字，它的字形像飞鸟从高处落到地上，其本义是到达。

The seal script of "至" is an associative compound, which means readers can understand its meaning by connecting the shape of the character. The character looks like a bird flying down from a high place and thus it means "arriving".

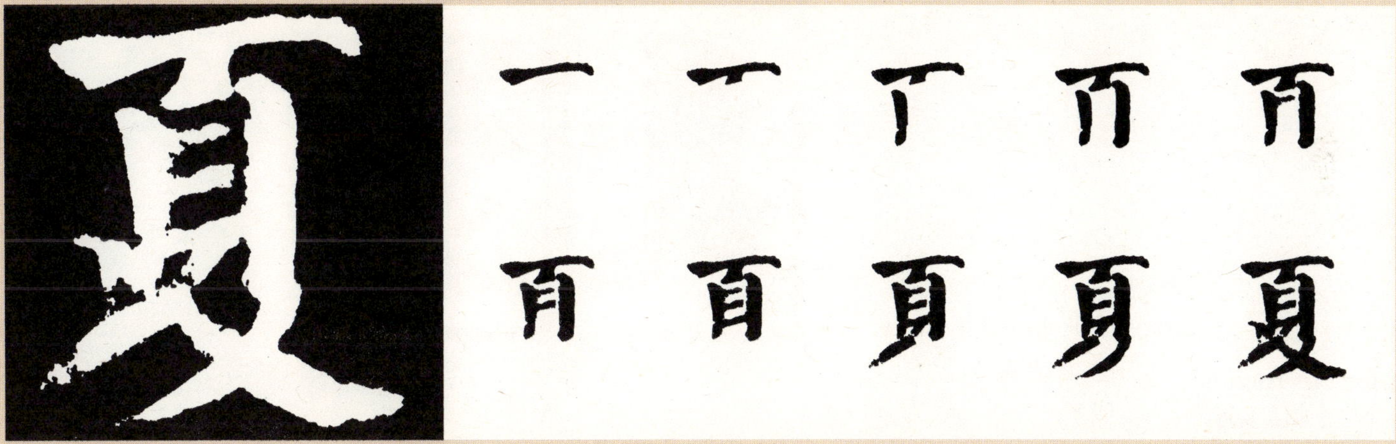
夏

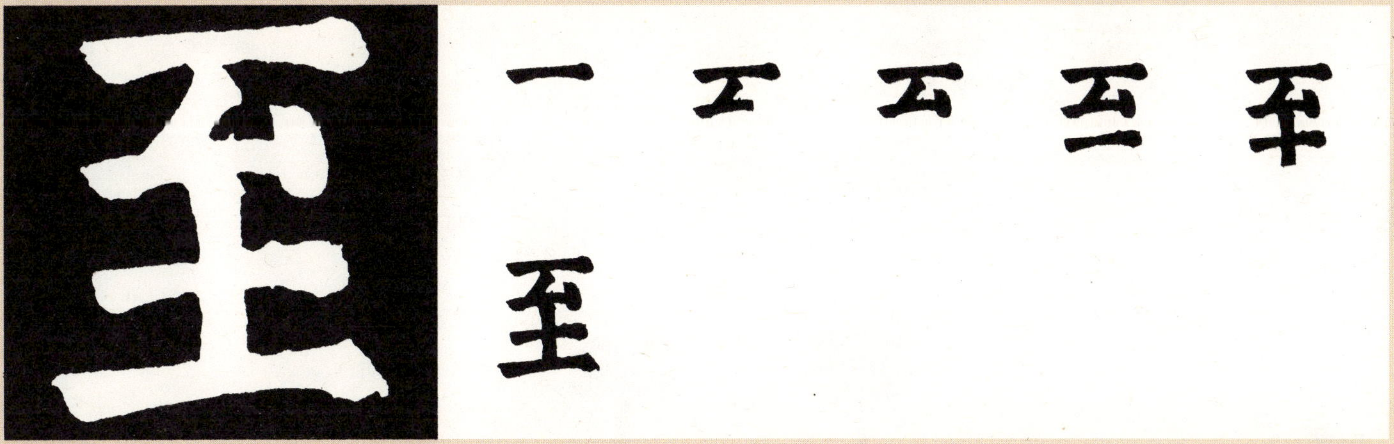
至

Make a gift with Chinese characters “夏至”

剪剪画画

做夏至的礼物

跟着妮妮和杰瑞做送给朋友的礼物

Let’s make some gifts for our friends with Nini and Jerry

剪一剪、画一画

Paper cutting and graphic design

Paper cutting by Nini
妮妮的剪纸

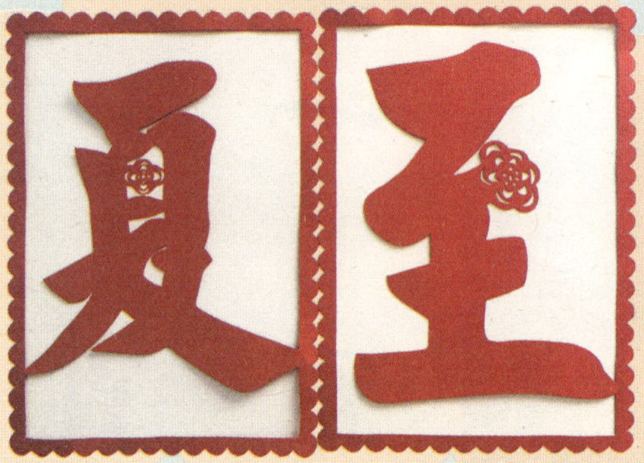

Graphic designed by Jerry
杰瑞的画

猜一猜、说一说

Let's make a guess

Let's make a guess with Nini and Jerry

与妮妮和杰瑞一起猜一猜

与“夏至”对应的是哪个星座？

Which astrological sign corresponds to Summer Solstice?

Let's have a competition with Nini and Jerry

与妮妮和杰瑞一起比赛

说出与“至”有关的词语

Try to say as many words as you can that are relevant to “至”

小暑

Lesser Heat

Xiao Shu

Important facts about Lesser Heat

The story of **Lesser Heat**

Lesser Heat, "Xiao Shu" in Chinese, comes between 6th and 8th July every year. Lesser Heat means that during this period of time it has already become hot, but the hottest days of the year haven't come yet. The Plum Rain season in the regions south of the Yangtze River begins to end and the hottest days of the year are about to arrive.

Changes after Lesser Heat

Heat wave scorches crops.

Crickets hide in the shades. Eagles fly high up in the sky.

Clothes are put in the sunlight and fresh air to get rid of the mold.

It is time to harvest and taste the new rice.

小暑的故事

小暑大事记

小暑的时间点在每年的7月6～8日之间。小暑是指这时的天气已经变得炎热，但还没有到一年中最热的日子。此时南方的梅雨季节即将结束，一年中最热的三伏天就要到来。

小暑变化

三伏起始，热浪滚滚。
蟋蟀居宇，鹰击长空。
衣物晒伏，品尝新米。

篆书（zhuan shu）| Seal script

篆书“小”字从字形上看像数颗细小的沙粒散落四周，表示细小、细微的意思。

The seal script of “小” resembles several tiny grains of sand scattered around, which indicates smallness or subtlety.

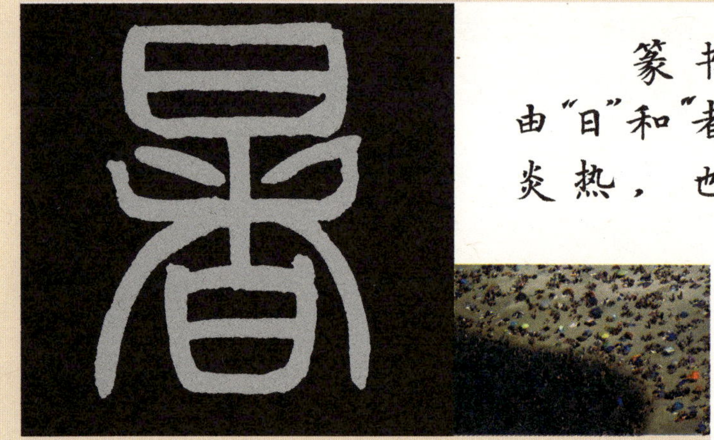

篆书“暑”字是上形下声，由“日”和“者”组成。它的本义是炎热，也指天气炎热的日子。

The seal script of “暑” consists of two characters “日”and “者”, with the upper part standing for the meaning and the bottom part standing for the sound. It originally means being extremely hot and also means the days with extreme heat.

楷书（kai shu）| Regular script

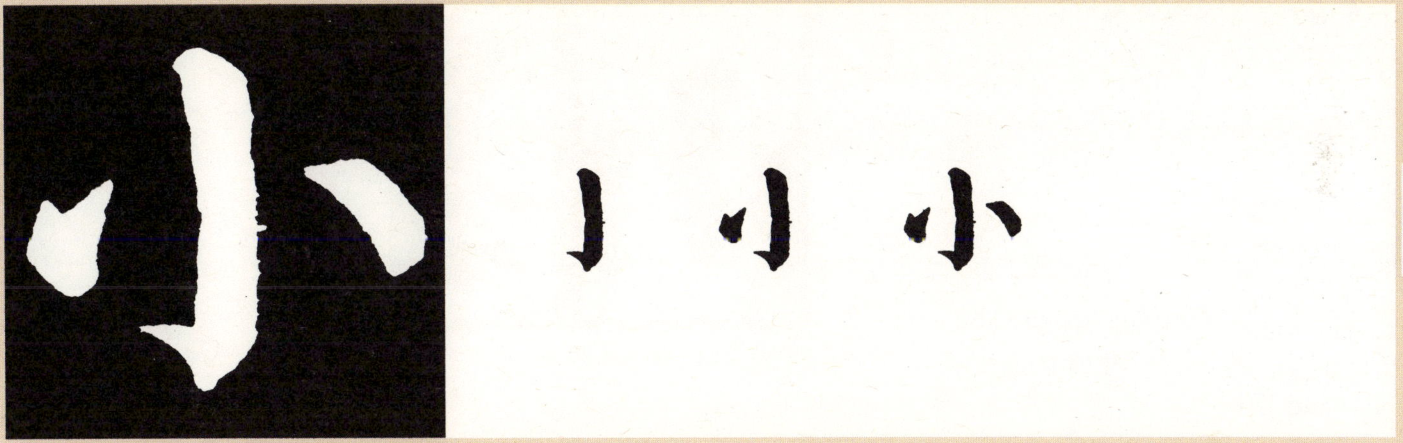

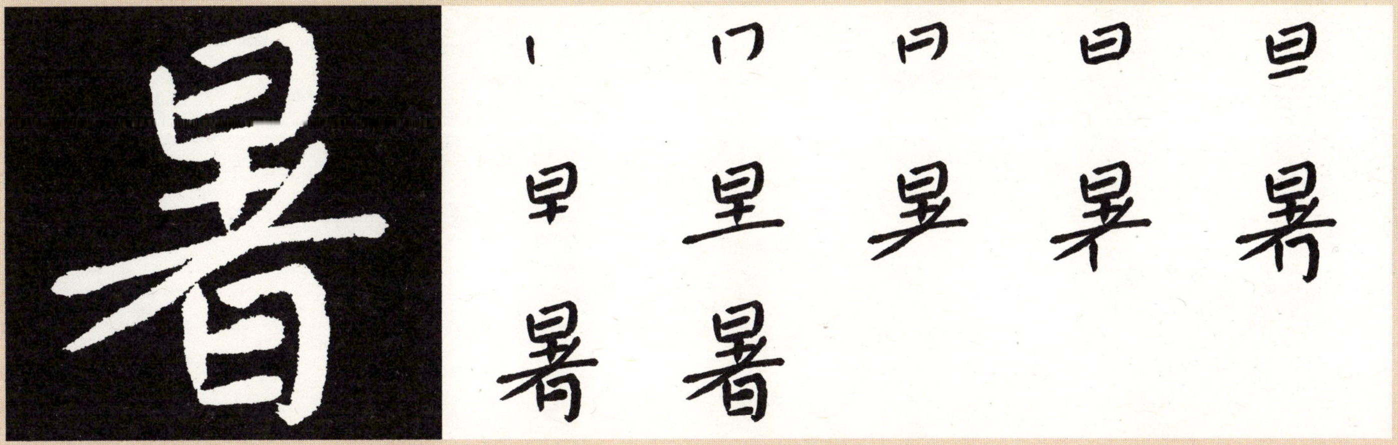

Make a gift with Chinese characters "小暑"

剪剪画画

做小暑的礼物

跟着妮妮和杰瑞做送给朋友的礼物

Let's make some gifts for our friends with Nini and Jerry

剪一剪、画一画

Paper cutting and graphic design

Paper cutting by Nini

妮妮的剪纸

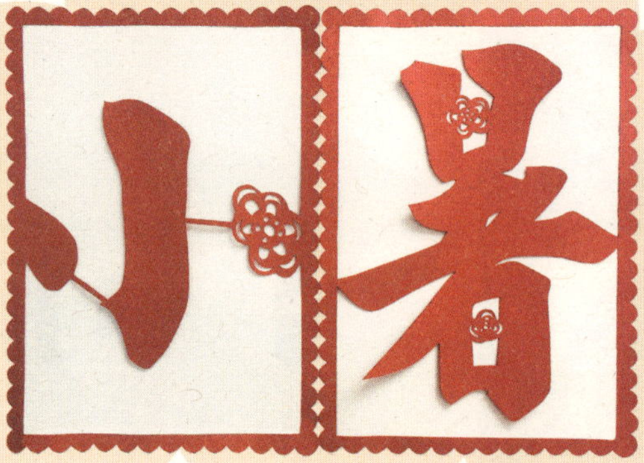

Graphic designed by Jerry

杰瑞的画

猜一猜、说一说

Let's make a guess

Let's make a guess with Nini and Jerry

与妮妮和杰瑞一起猜一猜

与"小暑"对应
的是哪个星座?

Which astrological sign corresponds
to Lesser Heat?

Let's have a competition with Nini and Jerry

与妮妮和杰瑞一起比赛

说出与"小"
有关的词语

Try to say as many words as you can
that are relevant to "小"

大暑

Greater Heat
Da Shu

The story of **Greater Heat**

Important facts about Greater Heat

Greater Heat, “Da Shu” in Chinese, is the last solar term of summer. It comes between 22nd and 24th July every year. Greater Heat is the hottest time of the Twenty-four Solar Terms. During this period of time, both the temperature and the daylight hours reach their peak of the year. Thunderstorms are frequent. It is also the fastest growing season for crops.

Changes after Greater Heat

Scorching hot temperature occurs.

The hottest time appears in the second of the three ten-day periods of the hot season.

Heavy rains sometimes pour. The soil gets wet and humid.

Fireflies fly around. The lotus is in blossom.

大暑的故事

大暑大事记

大暑是夏季最后一个节气，时间点在每年的 7 月 22～24 日之间。大暑是一年中最为炎热的时节，此时温度和日照时长都达到一年中的最高值，雷阵雨频发，这也是农作物生长最快的时节。

大暑变化

高温酷暑，热在中伏
大雨时行，土地潮湿
流萤纷飞，荷花开放

篆书 (zhuan shu) | Seal script

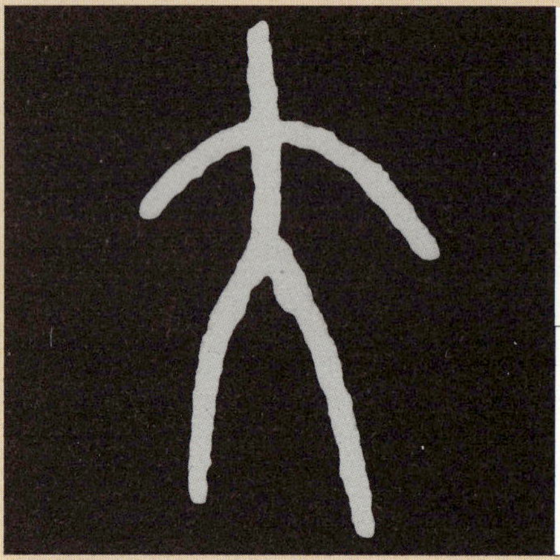

篆书"大"字像一个张开双臂和双腿的顶天立地的人。它的本义是天大，地大，人也大。

The seal script of "大" is like a man stretching out arms and legs to hold the heaven and the earth. It originally means the sky is wide, the earth is broad, and so is the human being.

篆书"暑"字是上形下声，由"日"和"者"组成。它的本义是炎热，也指天气炎热的日子。

The seal script of "暑" consists of two characters "日"and "者", with the upper part standing for the meaning and the bottom part standing for the sound. It originally means being extremely hot and also means the days with extreme heat.

跟着杰瑞写一写

Practicing calligraphy with Jerry

楷书 (kai shu) | Regular script

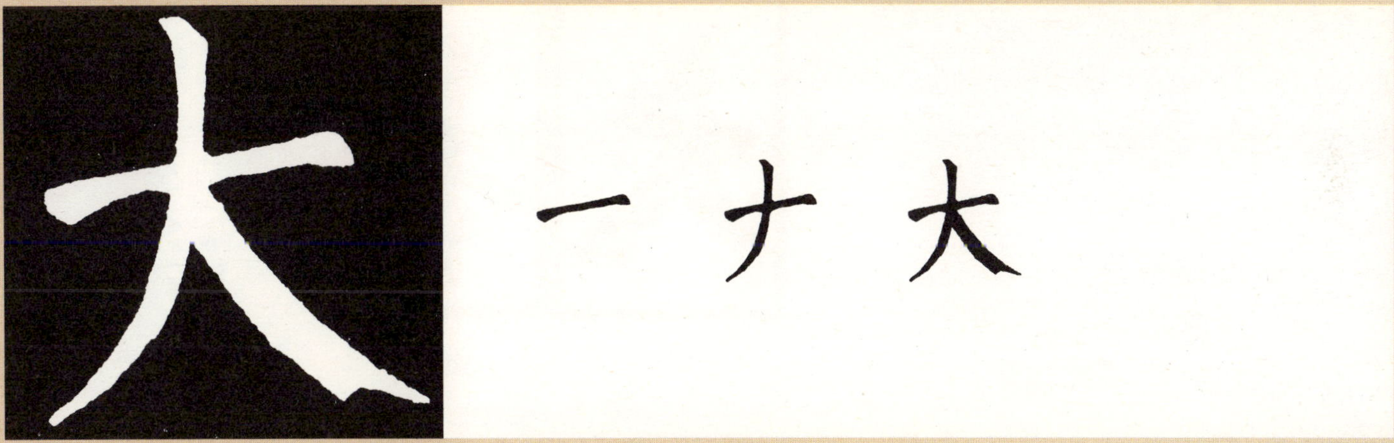

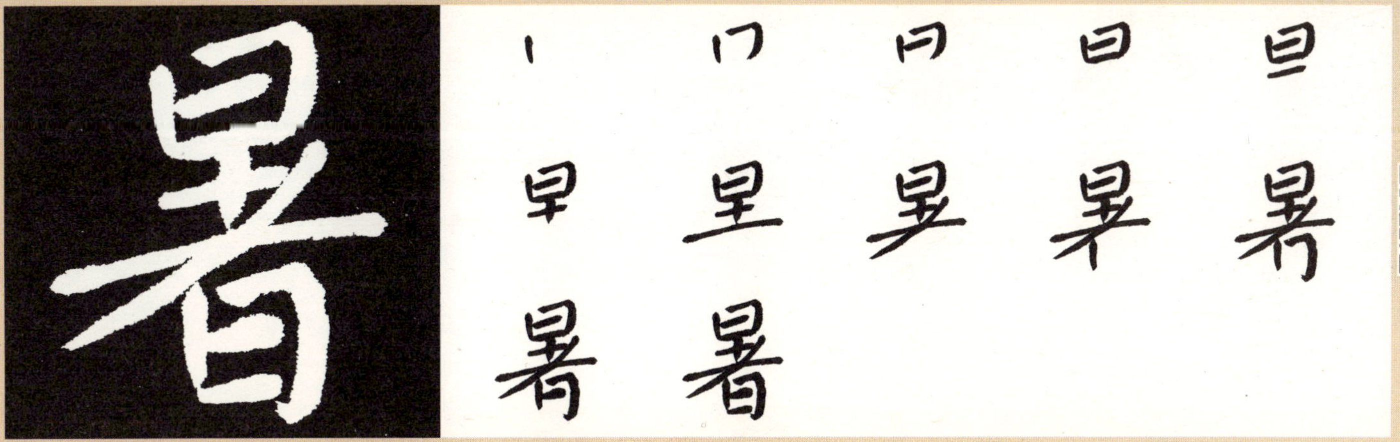

Make a gift with Chinese characters “大暑”

剪剪画画

做大暑的礼物

跟着妮妮和杰瑞做送给朋友的礼物

Let’s make some gifts for our friends with Nini and Jerry

剪一剪、画一画

Paper cutting and graphic design

Paper cutting by Nini

妮妮的剪纸

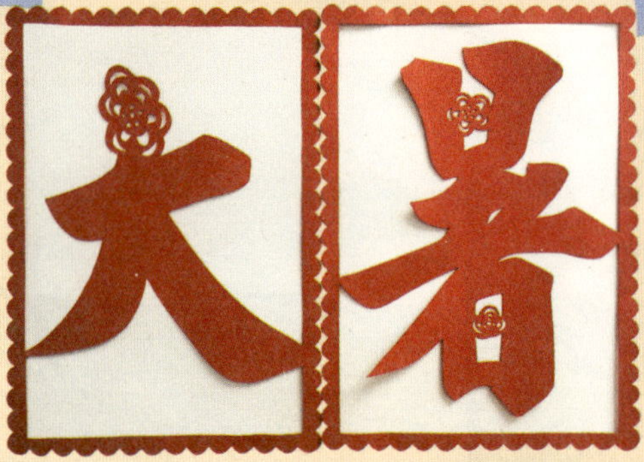

Graphic designed by Jerry

杰瑞的画

猜一猜、说一说

Let's make a guess

Let's make a guess with Nini and Jerry

与妮妮和杰瑞一起猜一猜

与“大暑”对应的是哪个星座？

Which astrological sign corresponds to Greater Heat?

Let's have a competition with Nini and Jerry

与妮妮和杰瑞一起比赛

说出与“大”有关的词语

Try to say as many words as you can that are relevant to “大”

后记

自2014年完成了"书法小联合国"文化特色教材《十二生肖我来写》之后，一直收到不同国家各级学校老师发来的邮件，询问是否可以买到课程的示范录像，也有老师与家长鼓励我继续编写一些有趣的关于中国传统文化的书法教材。

编写海外书法文化启蒙教材是一件十分艰难的事，看起来只是一本几十页的小书，要编写好绝非一日之功。首先要找到一个好的素材，之后要在不同的文化语境中反复进行教学实验，咨询各方专家的意见，最后方能定稿。多年来，"书法小联合国"国际系列教材编写的目标是：教材既要遵循受众国的文化习俗，又要在编写上做到准确、有趣，把中国故事讲好。

《风调雨顺：春夏秋冬》四册书法文化启蒙教材从酝酿到动笔撰写就花了近五年的时间，教材主要实验地在北美与南美部分学校，实验教材在使用过程中受到学生与教师的欢迎。该教材一方面介绍中国古代气象文化，以故事主人公中国妮妮给美国杰瑞讲故事的方式展开情节；另一方面，通过讲解汉字的构字特点来帮助不同文化背景的学生认知汉字里的文化，并采用二维码形式附上书法教学视频，方便实用，帮助学习者在书法、绘画、剪纸等艺术形式中加强对中国文化的整体理解。

感谢前联合国秘书长潘基文先生、上海交通大学张伟民教授、美国理海大学康妮教授、纽约大学唐力行教授、联合国国际学校孙青倩等老师在该教材编写过程中提出的中肯建议。感谢华东师范大学出版社王焰社长在教材出版过程中的大力支持。相信这四册“书法小联合国”汉字书法文化系列教材的顺利出版，会在中国书法文化国际教材开发中发挥积极的示范作用。

周斌于中国书法文化国际传播研究所

2017年10月28日

Postscript

Since the publication of *Let Me Write the Twelve Zodiac Signs* which belongs to the special course on calligraphy culture by United Association of Calligraphy in 2014, I have been receiving mails from parents and teachers from different schools all over the world. They asked me whether they could buy the video recordings of some demo lessons. And some of them encouraged me to keep writing more interesting calligraphy course books relevant to traditional Chinese culture.

It is not an easy task to compile a course book on calligraphy culture for overseas learners. Just as Rome was not built in a day, such a thin book of tens of pages also cannot be completed within a day. First of all, we need to find a suitable topic and its relevant materials. Then, we need to test the course book through continuous classroom instructions in various cultural contexts. After that we consult experts from all walks of life, and with feedback from classrooms, we finally make the decision to mass produce the course book. Our international course book series aim not only to suit the customs of the overseas learners but also to tell the stories of Chinese culture with accuracy and amusement.

From the blueprint to the first draft of the four course books — *Spring/Summer/Fall/Winter: Season with Timely Breeze and Rain for Crop Raising* — for the enlightenment on Chinese calligraphy culture, it took us nearly five years to present them to the public. These course books were put on trial mainly in some schools in North and South America and got very positive feedback from both teachers and students. This course book series introduces Chinese people's understanding of the climate in ancient time through stories told by a Chinese character named Nini to an American character named Jerry. Furthermore, we have selected some ancient Chinese characters to help students from different cultural backgrounds get a better appreciation of the culture of Chinese characters. Moreover, we have attached a QR code in the part Practicing Calligraphy with Jerry. If you scan the QR code, you can watch videos teaching you how to write the characters. Learners' comprehensive understanding of Chinese culture will be improved by learning and practicing Chinese calligraphy.

Here I want to extend my sincere gratitude to the former UN Secretary-General, Mr Ban Ki-moon; Professor Zhang Weimin from Shanghai Jiao Tong University, Professor Connie from Lehigh University, and Professor Lixing Tang from New York University for their pertinent suggestions during the process of compiling these course books. I'm also grateful to president of East China Normal University Press, Mrs Yan Wang, for her substantial support during the publication process. I firmly believe that the publication of these four course books would play a very positive role in the development of international course books on Chinese calligraphy culture.

Zhou Bin

In Chinese Calligraphy Culture Education and Communication Center

28th October 2017

图书在版编目（CIP）数据

风调雨顺. 夏 / 周斌，周佳楠主编. —上海：华东师范大学出版社，2018
ISBN 978-7-5675-7957-6

Ⅰ. ①风… Ⅱ. ①周… ②周… Ⅲ. ①汉语 – 对外汉语教学 – 语言读物 Ⅳ. ① H195.5

中国版本图书馆 CIP 数据核字（2018）第 144083 号

风调雨顺·夏

主　　编　周　斌　周佳楠
策划编辑　王　焰
责任编辑　曹　琛
特约审读　曹一凡
责任校对　张多多
封面设计　刘怡霖

出版发行　华东师范大学出版社
社　　址　上海市中山北路 3663 号　邮编 200062
网　　址　www.ecnupress.com.cn
电　　话　021-60821666　行政传真　021-62572105
客服电话　021-62865537　门市（邮购）电话　021-62869887
地　　址　上海市中山北路 3663 号华东师范大学校内先锋路口
网　　店　http://hdsdcbs.tmall.com

印 刷 者　上海盛通时代印刷有限公司
开　　本　700 × 1000　12 开
印　　张　7⅓
字　　数　50 千字
版　　次　2018 年 8 月第一版
印　　次　2018 年 8 月第一次
书　　号　ISBN 978-7-5675-7957-6/G · 11272
定　　价　48.00 元
出 版 人　王　焰

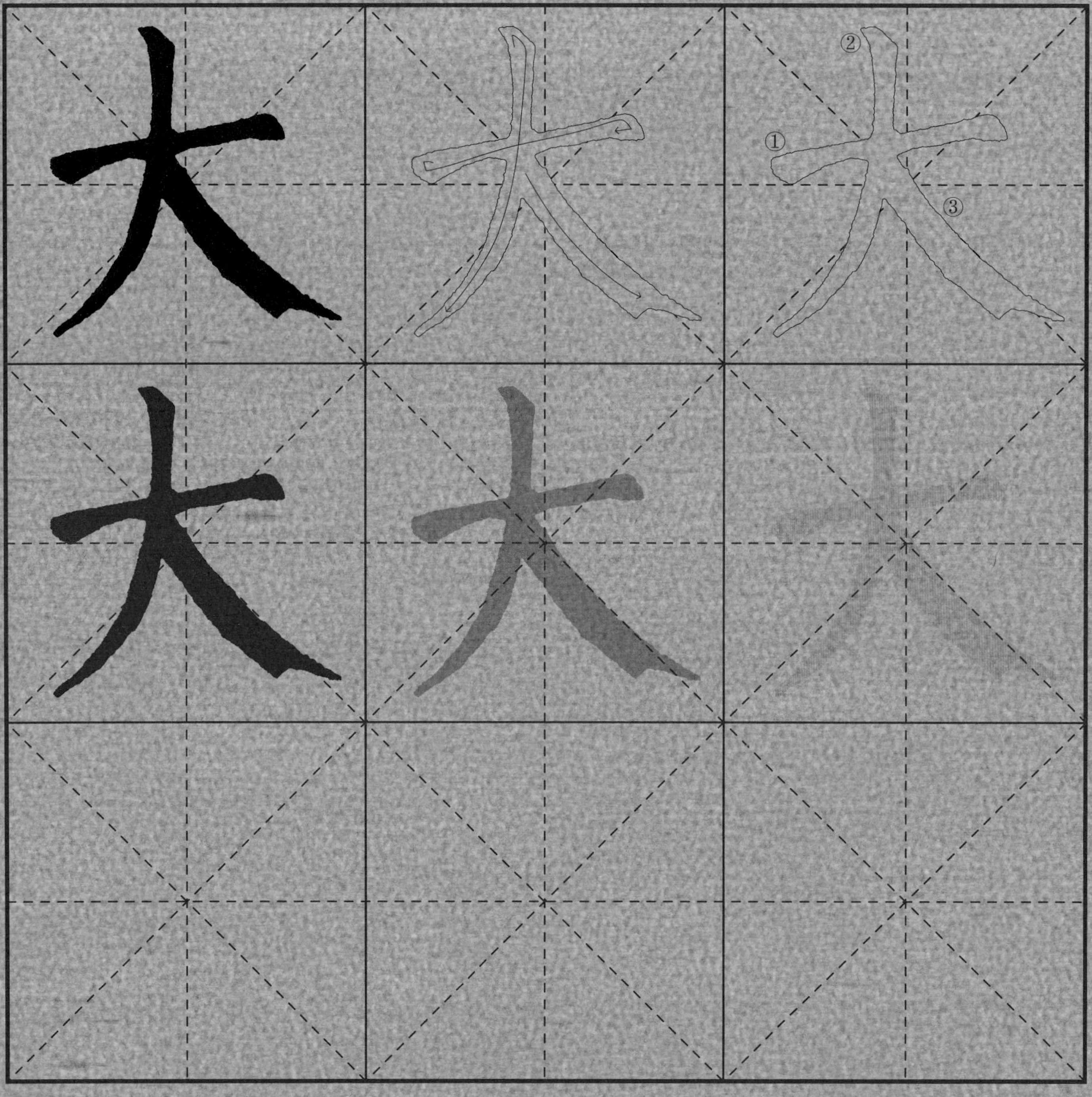
大
大
①
②
③
大
大
大
大

暑

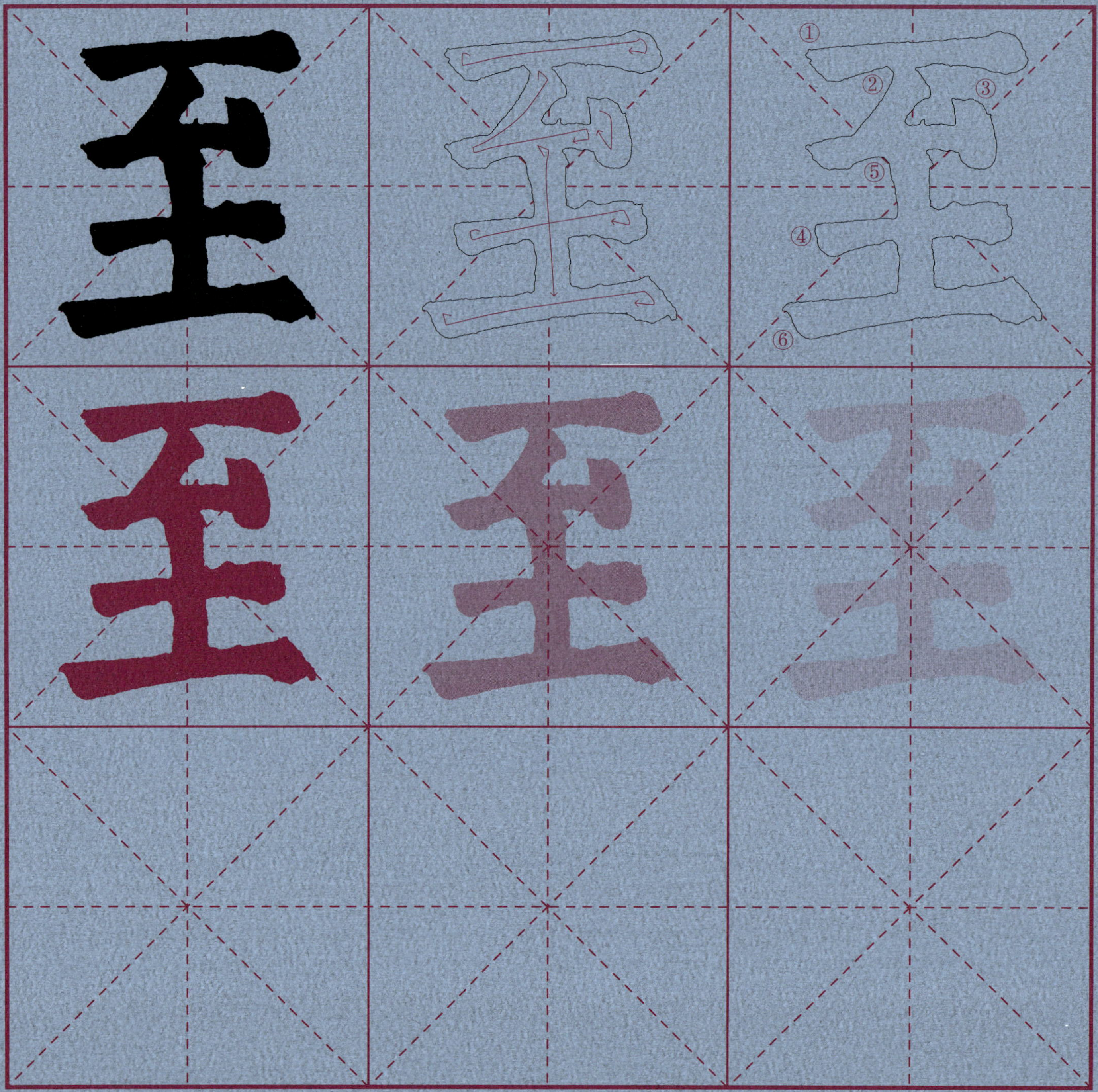
至 至 至
①②③④⑤⑥
至 至 至

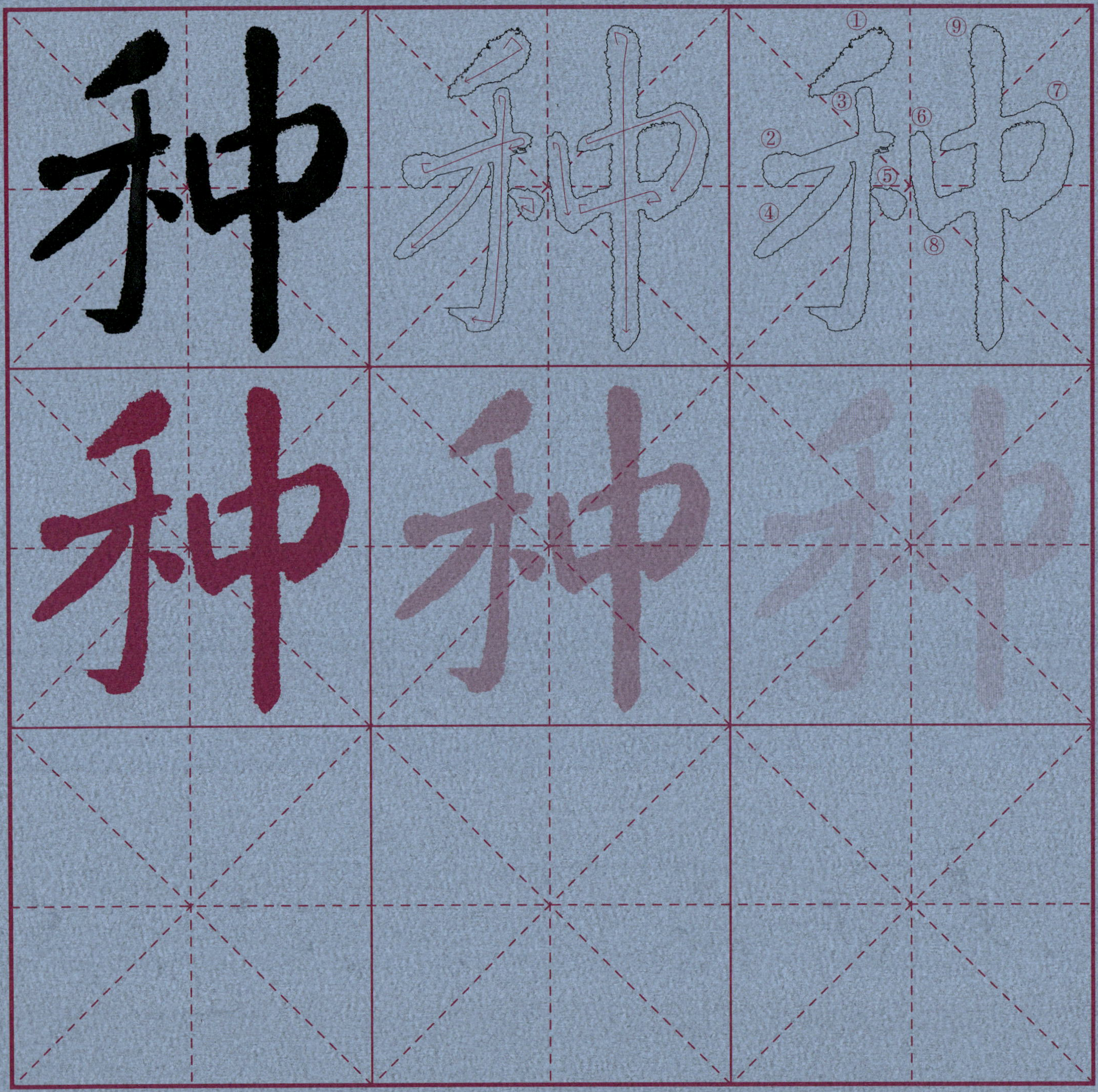
种

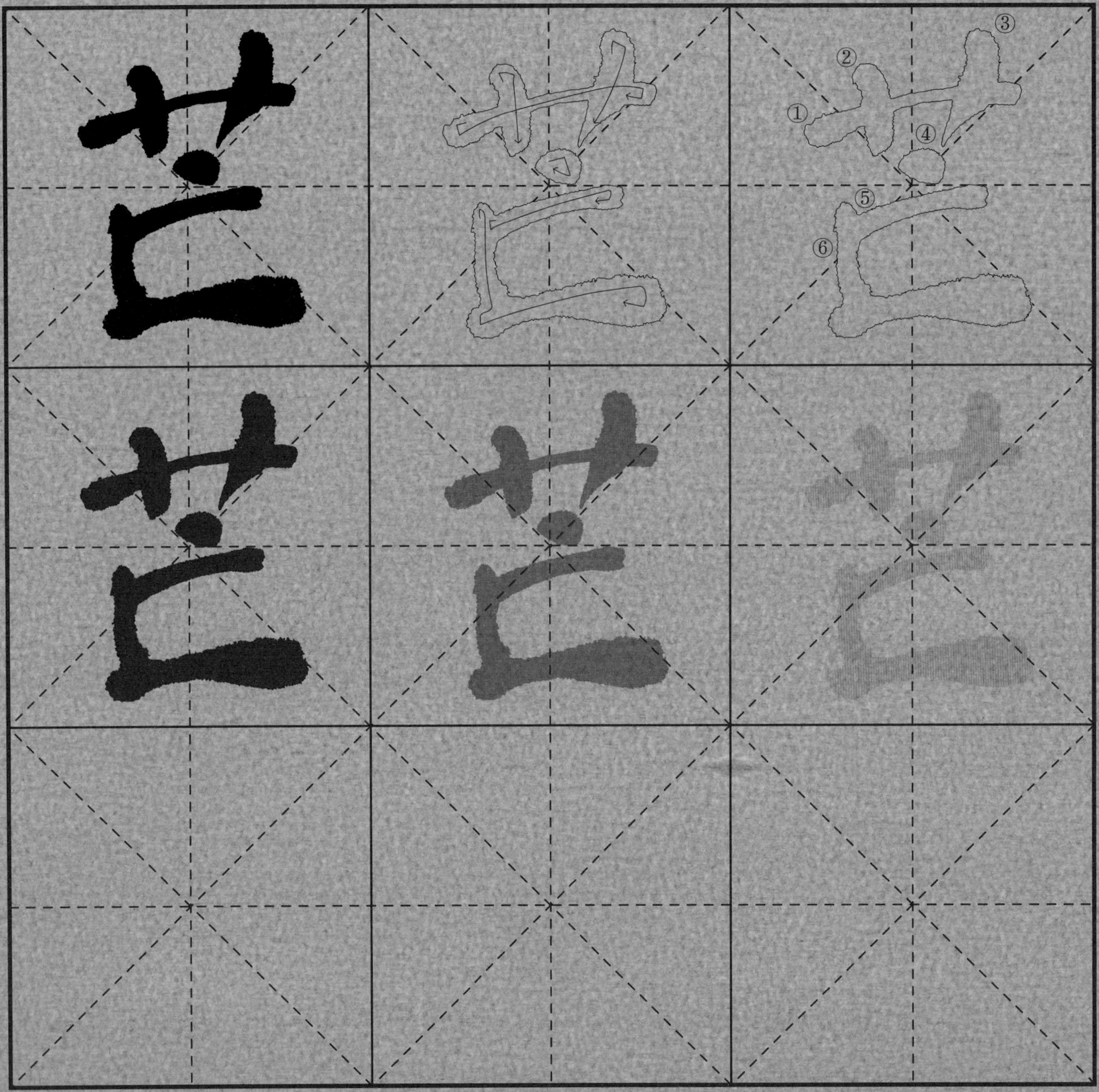
芒
①
②
③
④
⑤
⑥

滿

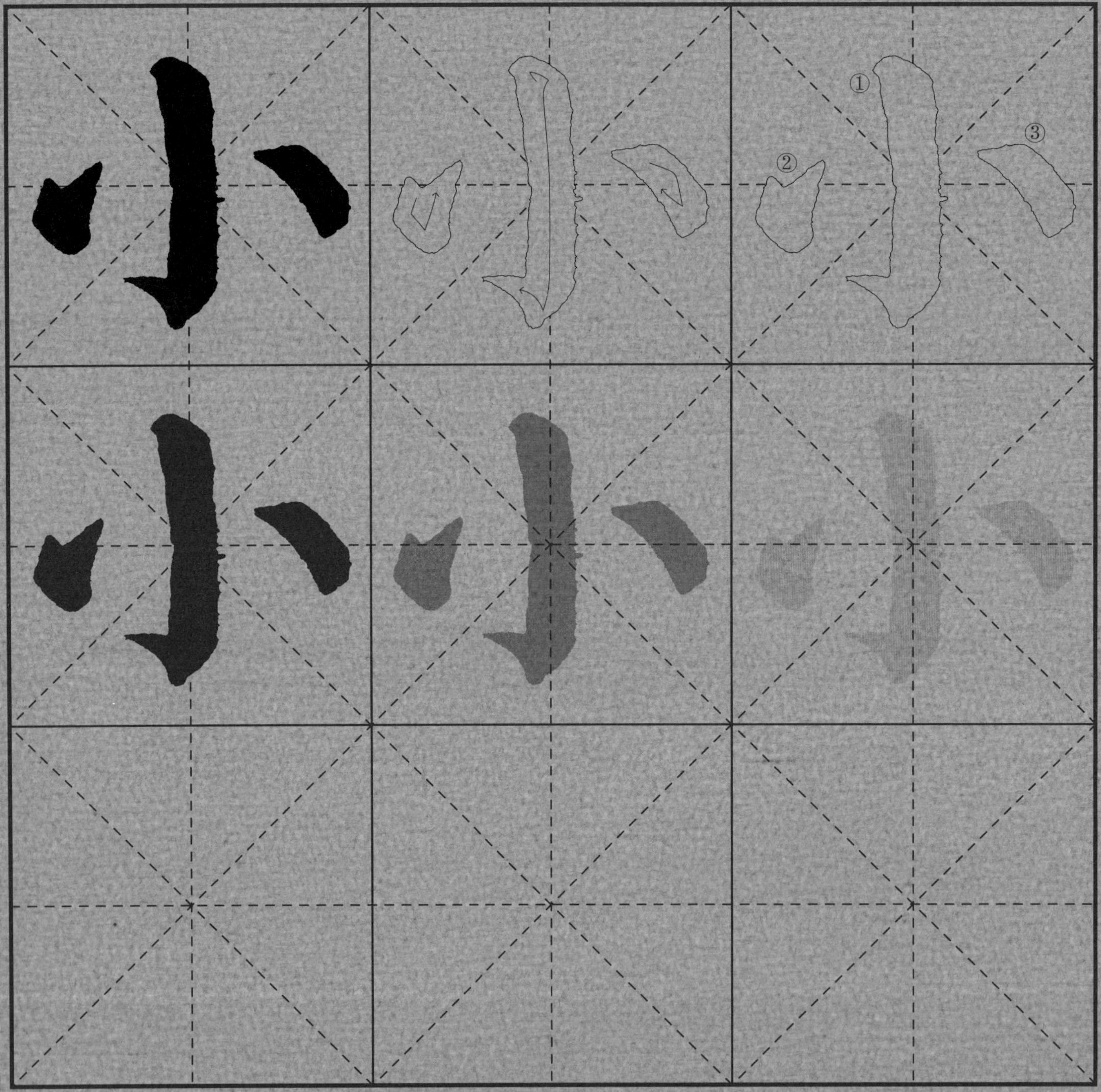
小
①
②
③

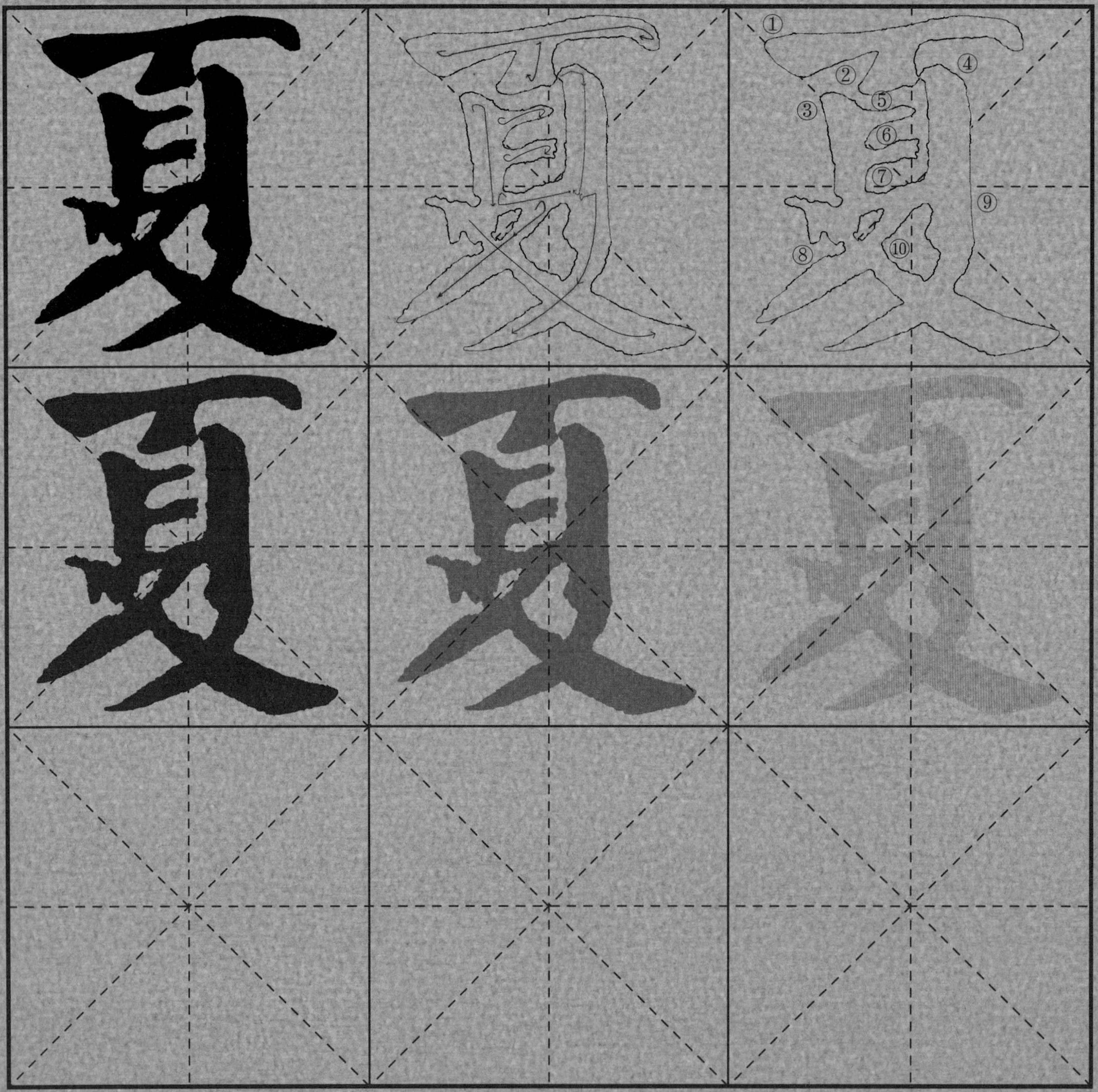
夏
夏
①
②
③
④
⑤
⑥
⑦
⑧
⑨
⑩
夏
夏
夏

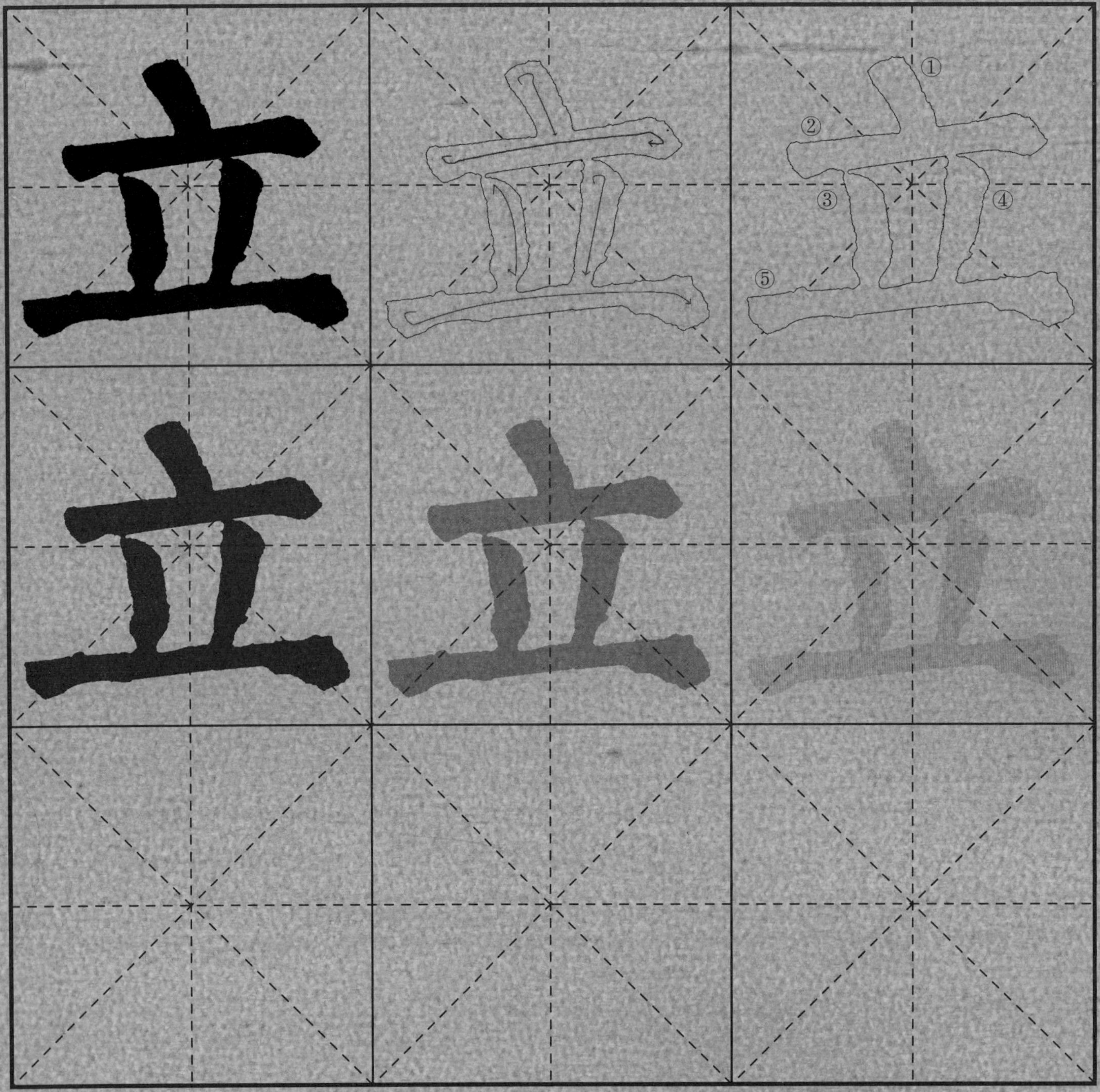
立
立
①
②
③
④
⑤
立
立
立
立